CHIMPANZEES

by Katie Marsico

Children's Press®

An Imprint of Scholastic Inc.
New York   Toronto   London   Auckland   Sydney
Mexico City   New Delhi   Hong Kong
Danbury, Connecticut

Content Consultant
Dr. Stephen S. Ditchkoff
Professor of Wildlife Sciences
Auburn University
Auburn, Alabama

Photographs © 2012: Bob Italiano: 44 foreground, 45 foreground;
Dreamstime: 2, 3 background, 44 background, 45 background
(Ian Maclellan), cover (Jens Klingebiel); Getty Images: 12 (Cyril
Ruoso/JH Editorial/Minden Pictures), 36 (Warwick Lister-Kaye);
iStockphoto: 16 (Eric Isselée), 40 (Mark Higgins); Minden Pictures/
Cyril Ruoso/JH Editorial: 7, 8; Photo Researchers/Martin Harvey:
27; Photolibrary/Clive Bromhall/OSF: 15; Shutterstock, Inc.:
1, 3 foreground, 19, 43 (Nick Biemans), 5 top, 23 (Sam DCruz);
Superstock, Inc.: 39 (Eye Ubiquitous), 5 bottom, 32 (IndexStock),
11 (Ingo Arndt), 4, 5 background, 20, 35 (Minden Pictures), 28,
31 (NHPA), 24 (Robert Harding Picture Library).

Library of Congress Cataloging-in-Publication Data
Marsico, Katie, 1980-
    Chimpanzees/by Katie Marsico.
        p. cm.—(Nature's children)
    Includes bibliographical references and index.
    ISBN-13: 978-0-531-20910-3 (lib. bdg.)
        ISBN-10: 0-531-20910-5 (lib. bdg.)
    ISBN-13: 978-0-531-21085-7 (pbk.)
        ISBN-10: 0-531-21085-5 (pbk.)
    1. Chimpanzees—Juvenile literature. I. Title.
    QL737.P96M365 2012
    599.885—dc23   2011037600

No part of this publication may be reproduced in whole or in part,
or stored in a retrieval system, or transmitted in any form or by any
means, electronic, mechanical, photocopying, recording, or otherwise,
without written permission of the publisher. For information regarding
permission, write to Scholastic Inc., Attention: Permissions Department,
557 Broadway, New York, NY 10012.
© 2012 Scholastic Inc.

All rights reserved. Published in 2012 by Children's Press, an imprint
of Scholastic Inc.
Printed in China 62
SCHOLASTIC, CHILDREN'S PRESS, and associated logos are
trademarks and/or registered trademarks of Scholastic Inc.

1 2 3 4 5 6 7 8 9 10 R 21 20 19 18 17 16 15 14 13 12

Chimpanzees

Class	Mammalia
Order	Primates
Family	Hominidae
Genus	*Pan*
Species	*Pan troglodytes*
World distribution	More than 20 countries in western and central Africa
Habitat	Primarily rain forests and savannas
Distinctive physical characteristics	Arms are long and muscular; body is mostly covered in long, black hair; flexible hands and feet feature excellent gripping abilities; forward-facing eyes; mouth has 32 teeth; opposable big toes
Habits	Able to "knuckle walk" along the ground but tend to spend much time in trees; social and belong to groups called communities or troops; occasionally migratory; territorial; capable of planning ahead and working together; able to create simple tools; intelligent and expressive of feelings and emotions
Diet	Eat about 80 different types of plant-based foods that include fruit, berries, nuts, seeds, buds, blossoms, and leaves; also feed on ants, termites, and small- to medium-sized mammals such as monkeys, wild pigs, and antelopes

Contents

6 | **CHAPTER 1**
Impressive Primates

10 | **CHAPTER 2**
Chimp Survival Skills

22 | **CHAPTER 3**
A Chimp's Life

29 | **CHAPTER 4**
Who Are These Apes?

37 | **CHAPTER 5**
Challenges to Chimps

42 | Words to Know

44 | Habitat Map

46 | Find Out More

47 | Index

48 | About the Author

Impressive Primates

No other animal **species** on Earth is as similar to human beings as the chimpanzee. These incredible **primates** share many behaviors with humans. They live in complex social groups and have many ways of communicating with each other. They even hug and kiss each other to show their feelings.

Chimpanzees, or chimps, are also highly intelligent. They can shape sticks, stones, and leaves into simple tools. People have even taught these amazing apes to use sign language!

Chimps and humans share certain physical characteristics. They both have **opposable** thumbs. They also have good eyesight and eyes that face forward.

Chimpanzees are some of the most intelligent and playful animals on Earth.

Where Do Chimps Live?

There are between 150,000 and 300,000 chimps living in the wild today. All of them live in Africa. They can be found in about 20 different African countries. But most chimps come from just two of them, Gabon and the Democratic Republic of Congo. Both countries are located in west-central Africa. They also share a border.

Chimpanzees usually make their homes in rain forests and savannas. Rain forests are forests that receive large amounts of rainfall. Savannas are flat, dry grasslands with few trees.

Chimps spend some of their time on the ground during daylight hours. At night, they rest in nests built high up in trees. Chimps build these nests out of twigs and branches.

 **FUN FACT!** Chimps sometimes adopt their younger brothers or sisters if their mother dies.

Chimps sleep in trees to stay safe from predators.

CHAPTER 2

Chimp Survival Skills

A chimp's most important tool for survival is its brain. Chimps are smart! They have developed survival skills that are too complicated for most other animals to learn.

They have learned how to turn a variety of objects into tools. For example, they sometimes use stones to smash open nuts. They use sticks to dig insects out of logs.

Chimps also use sticks to hunt small animals. They use their teeth to sharpen the sticks. They have been known to throw these sharp sticks like spears!

Termites are one of chimps' most important sources of food.

Other Signs of Intelligence

Chimps have proven that they have excellent memories. They are able to remember visual images in great detail. Scientists even think that these primates are able to plan ahead for certain situations and events.

Chimps use these abilities to come up with complex hunting plans. These plans often involve several members of a group working together to catch and kill **prey**. The chimps spread out over an area and use sounds to let each other know what is happening as they chase the prey. These hunting methods are often very successful.

 **FUN FACT!** A chimp named Washoe learned more than 240 different sign language signs.

Chimps work together to outsmart their prey.

A Mouth with Many Purposes

Chimps have 32 teeth that do a variety of jobs to help them survive in the wild. They are shaped much like human teeth. Their sharp **canines** are good for catching and killing prey. Their **molars** allow them to crush and grind up the tougher plants that they eat.

Chimps also use their teeth for things other than catching and eating food. They sometimes open their mouths to show off their teeth. But they are not smiling. Such behavior is often a method of warning enemies to keep their distance. If this doesn't frighten away the enemy, chimps can also use their teeth to defend themselves. Their painful bites can cause serious injury. Male chimps have larger canine teeth than females do. This is because the males use these teeth to fight each other.

An angry chimp is a frightening sight.

Sight, Hearing, and Smell

Chimps also have excellent vision. Their forward-facing eyes give them good depth perception. This means they can see how near or far away objects are. This is especially useful when they are swinging from tree to tree. Chimps are also able to see in color. This helps them tell if fruit is ripe or unripe.

Chimps hear about as well as humans do. They listen carefully to find out if enemies are nearby. They also listen to the sounds that other chimps make to communicate.

Chimps have a slightly better sense of smell than humans do. But they still rely far more on their eyes and ears than their noses!

 **FUN FACT!** Captive chimps enjoy listening to music. Some have even shown signs of having favorite songs or singers.

Like humans and many other primates, chimps have eyes that face forward.

Strong Bodies

Chimps have strong, **agile** bodies. They usually measure between 4 and 5.5 feet (1.2 and 1.7 meters) tall and weigh between 70 and 130 pounds (32 and 59 kilograms). A large chimp is about the size of a small adult human. But chimps are believed to be about four times stronger than an average human.

These powerful primates use their long, muscular arms to climb trees. Their shoulders are shaped in a way that allows them to swing from branch to branch. Chimps also use their strong arms to move along the ground. They can stand upright on two legs, but they usually walk on all fours. They support their weight on the knuckles of their hands. This type of movement is referred to as knuckle walking.

Most of a chimp's body is usually covered with long black hair. This keeps the chimp warm on cool African nights and protects it from harsh sunlight during the day.

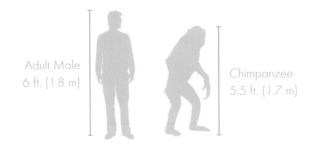

Adult Male
6 ft. (1.8 m)

Chimpanzee
5.5 ft. (1.7 m)

Chimps' long fingers allow them to walk on their knuckles.

Hands and Feet

Chimps can firmly grip many different objects with both their hands and their feet. Opposable thumbs allow them to grab things with their hands just as humans do. Opposable big toes allow them to do the same thing with their feet. Chimps can curl their big toes and touch them to the other toes. This allows them to grab on to objects such as tree branches. Grabbing branches with all four limbs allows them to travel very quickly through the treetops.

Like humans, chimps have very sensitive fingers and toes. They can feel temperature, texture, and pressure. Chimps also have fingernails and toenails to help protect them from injuries as they swing through the trees.

A chimp's toes and fingers lack the hair that covers most of the rest of its body. This allows it to get a better grip on tree branches and tools.

Grabbing branches with their feet allows chimps to free up their arms for carrying things.

CHAPTER 3

A Chimp's Life

Chimps spend much of their time looking for food. They feed on plants and other animals. Scientists believe that chimps eat about 80 different types of foods that come from plants. They especially like fruit. Chimps also **forage** for berries, nuts, seeds, buds, blossoms, and leaves. They find most of their food in trees.

Chimps eat meat, too. They hunt and kill **mammals** such as monkeys, wild pigs, and antelopes. The mammal they eat most often is the red colobus monkey. They also sometimes feed on insects such as ants and termites.

Chimps drink water by dipping leaves into rivers and ponds, and then sucking the water off the leaves. They understand that the leaves soak up water the same way a sponge would!

Chimps are omnivores, which means they eat both plants and animals.

Spending Time in a Troop

Wild chimps live in groups called communities or troops. Troops are made up of anywhere from a few dozen to 150 chimps. Troop members communicate with each other by making noises. They scream, grunt, and bang their hands on hollow trees. Chimps even make faces and use **gestures** to show what they are thinking.

Each troop controls a **territory**. The troop members protect the territory from other animals that try to steal their food or use their hunting grounds.

Males and females have their own social rankings within the troop. The alpha male and alpha female lead the other chimps in their troop. These chimps are often the strongest, largest members of the troop. The alpha male gets first choice of which females he will **mate** with.

Troop members have many ways of communicating with each other.

A Chimp's Childhood

Mother chimps usually have only one baby at a time. They give birth to live young about eight months after mating. An average baby chimp weighs about 4 pounds (1.8 kg) when it is born.

For the first month of its life, a baby chimp hangs on to its mother's stomach wherever she goes. After it grows a little stronger, it rides on her back. The baby shares a nest with its mother for several years. It drinks her milk until it is between four and five years old. The baby chimp and its mother share a close **bond** just as most human babies and their mothers do.

Young chimps are playful. They often tickle or chase each other. They laugh when they are happy or excited.

Female chimps are normally ready to mate when they are between 10 and 13 years old. Most males begin mating when they are between 12 and 15 years old. Chimps can live anywhere from 40 to 50 years in the wild.

Most baby chimps form close relationships with their mothers.

CHAPTER 4

Who Are These Apes?

Experts believe that chimps have existed for about six million years. This is roughly the same amount of time that humans have walked the earth.

Chimps are a type of primate called an ape. Other ape species include gorillas and orangutans. Chimps are smaller than most other apes. Scientists believe that chimps are also smarter than their ape relatives.

Monkeys are another type of primate. But they are not apes. Unlike apes, monkeys have tails. Monkeys are generally smaller than apes. They are also usually less intelligent than apes are.

Monkeys can use their tails to grab on to branches or other objects.

Similarities and Differences

Many scientists suspect that chimps are more like humans than they are like other apes! The similarities between people and chimps go beyond both species being able to use tools and communicate with sign language. Chimps are like humans because they have proven that they can feel and show emotions such as sadness and happiness. They also show affection in many of the same ways people do. Both chimps and human beings have long childhoods during which they bond with their mothers.

Of course, there are still big differences between chimps and humans. People do not look exactly the same as chimps. Humans are able to stand, sit, and walk upright more easily. Finally, chimps do not have a spoken language like people do.

Like humans, chimps often hug each other to show affection.

Different Types of Chimps

There are four main types of chimps. Masked chimps live in western Africa. Black-faced chimps live in the central part of the continent. Long-haired chimps live to the east. Nigeria-Cameroon chimps are named for the two countries where they are found. There are not many differences between these animals. They are mainly divided by where they live in Africa. Scientists say that all four groups are currently **endangered**.

 Newborn chimps have white tail hair that disappears as they get older.

Face color and hair length are two ways to tell types of chimps apart.

Bonobos

People used to think that there was a fifth type of chimp called the bonobo. But experts eventually decided that bonobos are a separate species altogether. Bonobos are thinner than chimps. They have smaller heads and ears. Their hair grows in different patterns. Bonobos also have an easier time walking upright than chimps do. Chimps live across a large stretch of western and central Africa. But bonobos are only found in a small part of the Democratic Republic of Congo.

Bonobos are even better at swinging through the trees than chimps are. They move faster and make longer jumps between branches. Some scientists believe that this is because of the bonobos' smaller size.

Bonobos are sometimes called pygmy chimps.

CHAPTER 5

Challenges to Chimps

Between one million and two million chimps lived in Africa during the early 1900s. But as human populations have grown since then, chimp populations have gotten smaller. There are now only about 150,000 to 300,000 chimps left in the wild. It is very possible that chimps could become **extinct** if people do not strengthen their **conservation** efforts.

Zoos make it possible for scientists to closely study chimps. Scientists can learn more about their health and behavior. They can then use this information to find new ways to help chimps survive in the wild. But it is important not to take too many chimps out of the wild and put them in zoos.

Scientists have an opportunity to study chimps up close in captive settings.

Predator Problems

The only three **predators** that chimps face are lions, leopards, and human beings. Today, humans are by far the biggest threat of the three.

Some people hunt chimps for food. Some chimp hunters can't find other things to eat. Other hunters sell chimp meat for high prices to people who want to try strange new foods. Many chimps are also captured and sold to zoos, circuses, laboratories, and pet stores.

People are destroying much of the chimps' **habitat** in Africa. As human populations continue to grow, they need more resources and more space. They cut down trees to collect wood for building materials and paper products. They also clear forests and swamps to create land for new farms and towns.

Cutting down trees leaves less space for chimps and other forest animals to live.

Helping Out

Many people are working to help prevent chimpanzees and other apes from going extinct. Some organizations work with the governments of many African nations to protect apes in national parks. They also encourage these governments to increase the size of protected areas and work harder to prevent illegal hunting.

There are researchers who study how chimps behave in the wild. Some people also work with small communities in Africa to teach local people about the importance of conservation. The locals are taught to avoid killing chimps or doing things that harm chimp habitats.

With the help of these people, chimps could get the chance to swing through the African wilderness for many years to come.

People will need to work very hard to make sure chimps continue to live and grow in their natural habitats for many more years.

Words to Know

agile (AJ-il) — able to move fast and easily

bond (BAHND) — a close connection with or strong feeling for someone

canines (KAY-nines) — pointed teeth located on each side of the upper and lower jaws

conservation (kon-sur-VAY-shuhn) — the act of protecting an environment and the living things in it

endangered (en-DAYN-jurd) — at risk of becoming extinct, usually because of human activity

extinct (ik-STINGKT) — no longer found alive

forage (FOR-ij) — search for food

gestures (JES-chuhrz) — actions that show feelings or thoughts

habitat (HAB-uh-tat) — the place where an animal or a plant is usually found

mammals (MAM-uhlz) — warm-blooded animals that have hair or fur and usually give birth to live young

mate (MAYT) — to join together to produce babies

molars (MOH-lurz) — wide, flat teeth at the back of the mouth used for crushing and chewing food

opposable (uh-POHZ-uh-buhl) — able to be placed opposite something else

predators (PREH-duh-turz) — animals that live by hunting other animals for food

prey (PRAY) — an animal that's hunted by another animal for food

primates (PRYE-mates) — any members of the group of mammals that includes monkeys, apes, and humans

species (SPEE-sheez) — one of the groups into which animals and plants of the same genus are divided

territory (TER-i-tor-ee) — area of land claimed by an animal

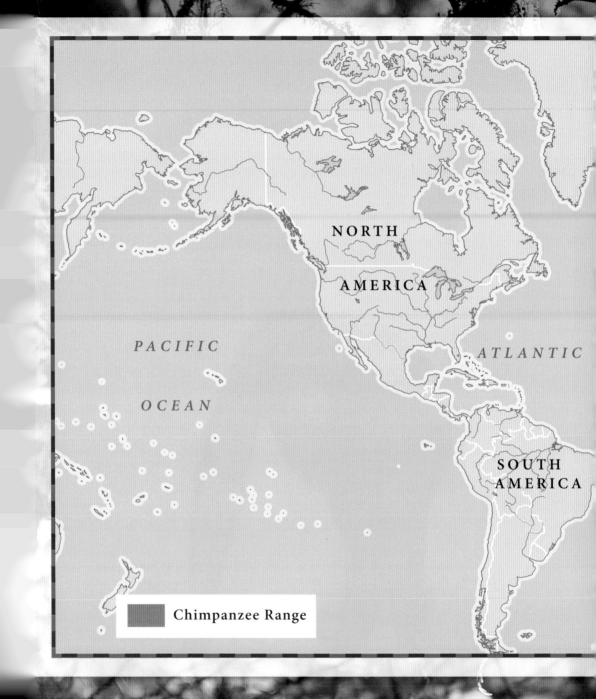

NORTH

AMERICA

PACIFIC

OCEAN

ATLANTIC

SOUTH
AMERICA

Chimpanzee Range

ARCTIC OCEAN

EUROPE

ASIA

AFRICA

INDIAN

OCEAN

OCEAN

AUSTRALIA

Find Out More

Books

Greenberg, Daniel A., and Christina Wilsdon. *Chimpanzees*. New York: Marshall Cavendish Benchmark, 2010.

Owen, Ruth. *Chimpanzees*. New York: Windmill Books, 2012.

Rockwood, Leigh. *Chimpanzees Are Smart!* New York: PowerKids Press, 2010.

Web Sites

Chimp Haven—Learn About Chimpanzees
www.chimphaven.org/kids-learn.cfm
Play games and find out how kids can help protect chimps.

National Geographic Kids—Chimpanzees
www.kids.nationalgeographic.com/kids/animals/creaturefeature/chimpanzee/
Check out photos, a video, and more information about chimps.

Visit this Scholastic web site for more information on chimpanzees:
www.factsfornow.scholastic.com

Index

affection, 30, 31
Africa, 9, 18, 33, 34, 37, 38, 41
apes, 29, 41
arms, 18, 20

babies, 26, 27
black-faced chimps, 33
bonobos, 34, 35

canine teeth, 14
colors, 17, 18, 32
communication, 6, 13, 17, 24, 25, 30
conservation, 37, 40, 41

defenses, 8, 14, 15

early primates, 28, 29
endangered species, 33
extinction, 37, 41
eyes, 6, 16, 17

feet, 21
females, 25, 26, 27
food. See plants; prey.
forests, 9, 38, 39

grip, 20, 21
groups. See troops.

habitats, 9, 18, 33, 34, 38, 39, 40
hair, 18, 21, 32, 33, 34

hands, 18, 21, 25
hearing, 17
height, 18, 18
hunting, 10, 13, 22, 25, 38, 41

intelligence, 6, 10, 11, 12, 13, 29

knuckle walking, 18, 19

legs, 18
lifespan, 26
long-haired chimps, 33

males, 25, 26
masked chimps, 33
mating, 25, 26
meat, 22, 38
milk, 26
molars, 14
monkeys, 22, 29

national parks, 41
nests, 8, 9, 26
Nigeria-Cameroon chimps, 33

opposable thumbs, 6, 21

people, 6, 17, 18, 21, 26, 29, 30, 37, 38,
        40, 41
plants, 14, 17, 22, 23
population, 9, 37

(Index continued)

predators, 38
prey, 10, 11, 12, 13, 14, 22, 25
pygmy chimps. See bonobos.

red colobus monkeys, 22

savannas, 9
scientists, 13, 22, 29, 30, 33, 34, 36, 37, 41
senses, 17
sign language, 6, 13, 30
sizes, 18, 18, 25, 29, 34
sleeping, 8
social rankings, 25
sounds, 13, 17, 24, 25

strength, 18, 25, 26
swinging, 17, 18, 21

teeth, 10, 14, 15
territories, 25
toes, 21
tools, 6, 10, 11, 21, 30
troops, 6, 12, 13, 24, 25

walking, 18, 19, 30, 34
water, 22
weight, 18, 26

zoos, 37, 38

About the Author

Katie Marsico is the author of more than 90 children's books. She has only seen chimps in zoos but hopes that people will do more to protect them in the African wilderness.